MW00836900

LIGHTNING
BOLT
BOOKS™

Pygmy Goats

Buffy Silverman

Lerner Publications ◆ Minneapolis

Lerner Publications Company
A division of Lerner Publishing Group, Inc.
241 First Avenue North
Minneapolis, MN 55401 USA

For reading levels and more information, look up this title at www.lernerbooks.com.

Library of Congress Cataloging-in-Publication Data

Names: Silverman, Buffy, author.
Title: Pygmy goats / Buffy Silverman.
Description: Minneapolis : Lerner Publications, [2017] | Series: Lightning
    bolt books. Little pets | Audience: Ages 6–9. | Audience: K to grade 3. |
    Includes bibliographical references and index.
Identifiers: LCCN 2017014144 (print) | LCCN 2017024361 (ebook)
    | ISBN 9781512483086 (eb pdf) | ISBN 9781512483031 (lb : alk. paper)
Subjects: LCSH: Pygmy goat—Juvenile literature. | Pygmy goats as
    pets—Juvenile literature.
Classification: LCC SF386.P94 (ebook) | LCC SF386.P94 S55 2017 (print) | DDC
    636.3/9—dc23
LC record available at https://lccn.loc.gov/2017014144

Manufactured in the United States of America
1-43324-33144-5/18/2017

Table of Contents

Meet the Pygmy Goat

Little goats play in a backyard. They jump and climb. They are pygmy goats!

Pygmy goats are as playful as puppies!

Pygmy goats look like goats on a farm. But pygmy goats are smaller. Adult pygmy goats weigh 50 to 85 pounds (23 to 39 kg). Farm goats may weigh 160 pounds (73 kg) or more.

An adult pygmy goat weighs about the same as a large dog.

Pygmy goats have beards under their chins.

Pygmy goats have horns on top of their heads. Male goats grow longer horns than female goats. Goats butt heads with one another to play and to show other goats which one is the boss.

Goat horns could get stuck in fences. People may remove a pygmy goat's horns from its head for safety. Always talk to a vet before deciding whether to have a goat's horns removed.

A Pygmy Goat Is Born

A female pygmy goat calls loudly. *Meeehh! Meeehh!* She is giving birth to a baby.

A baby goat is called a kid. The mother pygmy goat licks her kid clean.

The mother gives birth to one to four kids. People wipe the kids' mouths and noses. They make sure the kids can breathe.

Kids grow for five months inside their mother.

A little kid struggles to its feet. It searches for its mother's teat. The kid drinks milk from the teat. A mother's milk has nutrients to keep a kid healthy.

Kids begin looking for their mother's teat as soon as they can stand.

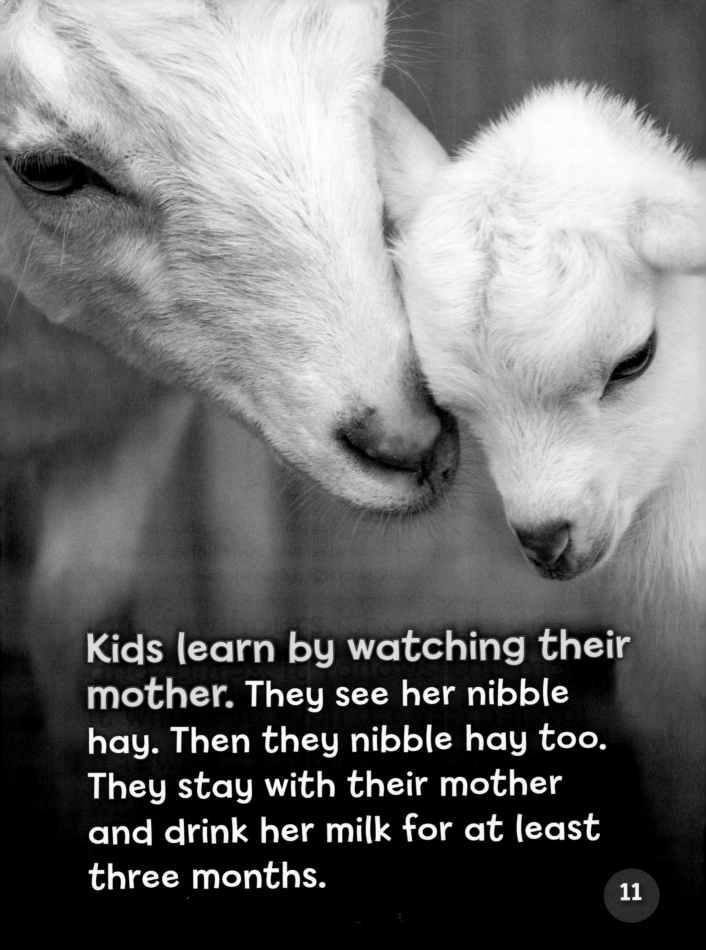

Kids learn by watching their mother. They see her nibble hay. Then they nibble hay too. They stay with their mother and drink her milk for at least three months.

Pygmy Goat Life

Wild goats are herd animals. That means they live in groups with other goats. A pygmy goat pet should live with at least one other pygmy goat.

Pygmy goats live together outside. They eat grass and chomp weeds.

Some pygmy goats are nervous when they meet new people. The goats learn to not be afraid. Goats get used to people who sit quietly.

A pygmy goat wags its tail when it is excited. It may butt you with its head to get your attention.

Pygmy goats jump and kick.
They chase one another. They
climb and play.

Caring for a Pygmy Goat

Pet pygmy goats need a yard with a strong fence to stay safe. They are good jumpers and climbers. The fence must be tall enough to keep the goats inside.

A shed keeps pygmy goats dry in rain or snow.

Some pygmy goats are picky eaters. Others will eat almost any plant. People make sure goats can't reach poisonous plants. Pygmy goats eat vegetables, hay, and special feed.

Pygmy goats need special care. People trim their hooves. A vet checks pygmy goats for parasites.

A vet makes sure a pygmy goat is healthy.

Pygmy goats live for about ten years.

Pygmy goats are safe inside their shed. Their owner brings them food. The goats sleep on straw beds. Good night, pygmy goats!

Pygmy Goat Diagram

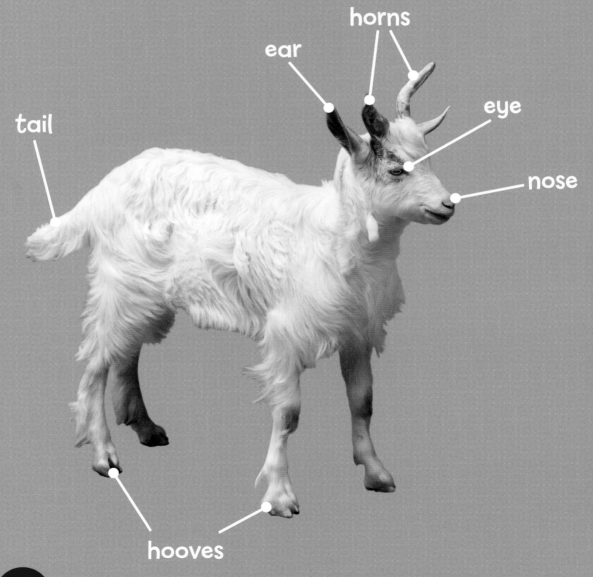

tail

ear

horns

eye

nose

hooves

Fun Facts

- Pygmy goat mothers make milk for their kids. People also enjoy goat milk. They drink the sweet milk or make goat cheese.

- Not all pygmy goats sound alike! Scientists have found that kids that are raised together sound like one another. Their sound is different from pygmy goats in other herds.

- Pygmy goats have no upper teeth in the front of their mouths. They have a hard pad instead of teeth. They use the pad to help pull grass into their mouths.

Glossary

butt: strike with the head

feed: solid animal food

herd: a group of animals that live together

hoof: a thick covering that protects the feet of goats. The plural of *hoof* is *hooves*.

nutrient: a substance in food that keeps an animal healthy

parasite: a living thing that lives on and gets its food from another living thing

teat: part of a goat through which milk flows

vet: a doctor who cares for animals. *Vet* is short for *veterinarian.*

Further Reading

How to Care for Pygmy Goats
http://www.wikihow.com/Care-for
-Pygmy-Goats

Kenney, Karen. *Pygmy Goat*. Vero Beach, FL: Rourke Educational Media, 2016.

Owings, Lisa. *From Goat to Cheese*. Minneapolis: Lerner Publications, 2015.

Pets 101—Pygmy Goats
https://www.youtube.com/watch?v=J3fxgi7F_qI

Pygmy Goat
http://www.oregonzoo.org/discover/animals
/pygmy-goat

Wood, Alix. *Pygmy Goats*. New York: Windmill Books, 2017.

Index

Photo Acknowledgments

The images in this book are used with the permission of: Eric Isselee/Shutterstock.com, p. 2; schubbel/Shutterstock.com, p. 4; marc macdonald/Alamy Stock Photo, p. 5; Wolfgang Zwanzger/Shutterstock.com, p. 6; Jaboticaba Fotos/Shutterstock.com, p. 7; Russotwins/ Alamy Stock Photo, p. 8; Mark Andrews/Alamy Stock Photo, p. 9; ANURAKE SINGTO-ON/Shutterstock.com, p. 10; Dawna Moore/Alamy Stock Photo, p. 11; Targn Pleiades/ Shutterstock.com, p. 12; © Nick Upton/Minden Pictures, p. 13; Darla Hallmark/Shutterstock. com, p. 14; David & Micha Sheldon/F1online digitale Bildagentur GmbH/Alamy Stock Photo, p. 15; YuliiaKas/Shutterstock.com, p. 16; Vishnevskiy Vasily/Shutterstock.com, p. 17; © Jose Manuel Gelpi Diaz/Dreamstime.com, p. 18; Barry Hitchcox/Alamy Stock Photo, p. 19; Vladimir Wrangel/Shutterstock.com, pp. 20, 22.

Front cover: CEW/Shutterstock.com.

Main body text set in Billy Infant regular 28/36. Typeface provided by SparkType.